STILLWATER TROUT FLY-FISHERS' READY REFERENCE

by

PETER LIGHTFOOT & KEVIN WHAY

A WATERSIDE HANDBOOK

Published by SPRINGWATER PUBLICATIONS,
23 Cable Road, Hoylake, Wirral. L47 2AY.
051-632 1888

1st Edition 1985
2nd Edition 1986

To our long-suffering and ever-loving wives, without whose help this book would have been written twice as quickly . . . .

ACKNOWLEDGEMENTS

With many thanks . . . .

to John, Peter & Joyce Percival, and all at Meadow Fishery, Mickle Trafford, Cheshire, for fine fishing, good company and endless patience.

to Ken Hopkins of Ken Hopkins Sports, Moreton, Wirral, for tying the flies illustrated. Fly-tier and raconteur extraordinaire . . . !

to Paul Williams, for his help and invaluable advice.

to John A. Parkes, New Ferry, Wirral, for his assistance in the beginning.

to Mike Fletcher, Barnston, Wirral, for his assistance at the end.

PHOTOGRAPHS BY BILL FERRIE

CONTENTS

INTRODUCTION

The prime purpose of this READY REFERENCE is to help you catch more fish.

Its aim is to act as a guide to enable you to choose quickly and simply the right fly for the moment, to give a general understanding of its usage, and to help form the basis of a fly collection.

When standing by the waterside watching a 5lb. trout cruising up and down, you don't necessarily want a stack of books by your side to thumb slowly through for ideas; nor do you really require to know that a Goëra Pilosa is a Medium Sedge with a patch of hair on the anterior wing; nor, having eventually found the fly you think will suit, do you need it cross-referenced on pages 46/47; 59/60, 135/136!!! No. What you want is very quickly to find the fly that will do the job and get stuck into the fish . . . .

This READY REFERENCE should help you do just that. It is an accumulation of our experience and that of many fishermen we have encountered, together with information gleaned from the volumes of literature we have 'waded' through. It condenses all those myriad droplets of thought and knowledge into useful and usable information. The thousands of different artificial flies that have been tied are trimmed down to an essential, well known and readily available selection. These are capable of catching 95% of trout — the remaining 5% will be left for those days when even a depth charge won't bring them out.

—BUT THAT'S FISHING!!!

HINTS AND TIPS

THE FISH

There are only a few types that interest the stillwater trout angler. A brief description is necessary, because it's nice to know what you've landed. More importantly, it's nice to know if you can keep it, because if it's out of season, back it goes!

The easiest way to find which fish are in season is to ask at the time you purchase your licence and/or permit for the waters you have chosen.

Descriptions:—

BROWN TROUT

The only trout native to our waters. Generally speaking they have pronounced spots, often some red, but with no spots on the tail or fins. The colour is basically mid-brown with a yellowish underbelly, but this of course can vary from region to region.

RAINBOW TROUT

An American immigrant that now provides the majority of our stillwater fly-fishing. These often have a vivid band of purple/mauve that virtually follows the lateral or mid-line of the fish. They have an abundance of spots on the body as well as on the fins and tail. They normally have white underbelly and a greyish-green back.

AMERICAN BROOK TROUT

Another American immigrant. Clearly recognisable being olive green to the upper part of the body with 'dappled' effect markings and few spots. The lower part of the body and fins are white with an orange/red tinge and the white fore-edges of the fins make the fish unmistakeable.

HYBRIDS:—

TIGER TROUT

A cross between an American Brook Trout and a Brown Trout. It has a 'squiggly' dappled effect to the upper part of its body (obviously from the Brook Trout but much tighter in design), and also displays white fore-edges to the lower fins.

CHEETAH TROUT

A Brook Trout and Rainbow Trout cross. Described as 'dappled with blotches' although looking more like the Rainbow than the Brookie.

TRIPLOIDS

Genetically produced Rainbows which are, in effect, sexless. Virtually indistinguishable from normal Rainbows.

ALL-FEMALE FISH

Another genetically produced Rainbow which is indistinguishable apart from the larger size to which it can grow.

OUT OF CONDITION FISH

During certain times of the year trout can go into 'breeding fettle'. When this occurs, cock fish can turn almost black with a pronounced 'hooked' lower jaw, whilst the hen fish turn a greyish-black on the underbelly. In this condition they can taste rather 'muddy' and should really be returned to the water to let them get on with what nature intended! Although rainbow trout do not successfully breed in any quantity when released in Britain, they can go through the motions!

THE CONFIDENCE

. . . The single most important item an angler needs. Without this essential requirement, many fish otherwise taken, will be lost.

When a fisherman is confident, it exudes from him, travels down the line and into the fly, transmitting a 'come and get me' message to the patrolling trout looking for an easy meal. This, at least, is the mystical element of confidence.

The practical element means that you are alert, concentrating on every cast, watching for the slightest take and being aware of every change in fishing conditions.

It's hard to remain confident after a day's thrashing at the water with no result. It's at times like this your mind switches off, your eyes gaze dreamily into the horizon and casting becomes a reflex action. About an hour before your time is up, the next stage sets in — panic. Everything is tried until finally the largest lure is stripped fast through the water in the hope that the speed will frighten the fish into taking . . . . . .

Confidence is lost!

One of the finest cures for this condition is to choose and fish your favourite fly, the one you have greatest faith in. By doing so you believe you have a chance of catching and therefore tend to concentrate harder; your mind begins to work logically again, and you think about what you're doing . . . . . .

Confidence is restored!

THE QUESTIONS

Ask lots. Especially if you go to a stillwater you haven't fished before. Ask as many fishermen (and especially the locals who fish there regularly) such questions as:—

"Where are the best spots?"

"What's the best fly to use at the moment?"

"What flies are hatching?"

Fishermen are usually a gregarious bunch and will be more than willing to help and advise.

It never ceases to amaze us how some fishermen refuse to ask a more successful angler what method and catching pattern he is using. If it's a case of pocketing one's pride — then pocket it — and catch more fish!

THE OPTICS

Not the ones you see in a bar, but the ones you look out of, your eyes. Eye protection is the name of the game when it comes to fly-fishing. You can cast anything up to 500 times during a day, sometimes more. One mistake, one awkward gust of wind, and the fly's in your eye, hook and all.

If you wear glasses, then wear them. If you don't, then wear sunglasses, and always of the polarised variety. These glasses can be bought with clear, as well as dark lenses, for those all too many dull days, this includes clip-ons for spectacle wearers.

Apart from the obvious advantage of eye protection, polarised glasses cut through surface glare and enable you to see into the dark, cool depths to search out thc fish. The hunt is on . . . .

THE HUNT

Fly-fishing is hunting. It's searching out your quarry rather than just dangling a worm and waiting for the fish to come to you.

It means moving and scanning. All too often, anglers arriving at a stillwater, grab the nearest available spot and start casting out blindly.

It's far more productive to give the lake a hard looking at, moving around it slowly, keeping your eyes and ears wide, searching for a rise, or any sign of fish movement, and listening for tell-tale splashes.

Do all this before you even consider casting. Because when you do start, you'll have chosen the best area.

THE RISES . . .

Or why trout jump from the water and what to do about it.

Trout jump, or rise, for two main reasons. The first, because they feel like it, the second, for food!

If a trout leaps for no apparent reason, for example, in the middle of a downpour, when there is no obvious hatching, then it's probably doing it for its own, obscure trouty reasons. It could, of course, be trying to escape a hungry pike, in which case it has every right to do so.

The rises that interest us are those connected with food. These types of rise can be sub-divided into numerous different patterns, but they all boil down to either a slow rise or a fast one.

A slow rise, where the fish are 'head and tailing', cruising just sub-surface, 'sipping' the surface, creating slow 'V' wakes, or 'bulging' the water without actually showing, indicates that the fish is in no particular hurry and that the fly, or food, must be relatively slow moving, such as Midge Pupae, snails and spent flies.

A fast rise, where trout are leaping frantically from the water or roaring through the surface like demented speedboats, show that the food is ultra mobile like Sedge Pupae, Caenis, Damselfly Nymph or Fish Fry, Sticklebacks and Minnows.

Try to judge the situation as it happens and choose the artificial fly accordingly. Suitable patterns will be found in the Artificial Fly Section.

THE SPOON

When you catch and keep a fish always spoon it with a marrow scoop to see what it's been taking. You can often be surprised; the fish you thought was feeding on sedge pupae could well have been eating minnows.

By spooning the fish you can select the appropriate artifical pattern to match the genuine food item.

THE LINES & LEADERS

There has been much speculation and argument as to the correct colour of a fly-line. Some swear by bright, day-glo orange, while others use dull brown. We believe the fish will spot the line no matter how you try to disguise it — whether it be with pink spots or zig-zag stripes!

What they do is tend to ignore it, so use a line with a colour you can see, that way you'll spot the 'takes' more easily.

The leader, or tippet, or cast, as it is variously known, presents a different problem. A large lure, stripped fast, will tend to obscure the leader as everything is moving at speed. If you use a 10lb (4.5 Kg) leader with a size 16 Grey Duster, instead of the fly alighting gently on the water like a single snowflake, it will dive-bomb the surface like a Kamikaze pilot. Under these circumstances, there is no doubt that the leader is highly visible to the fish.

The finer the line, the less likely it is to be seen. For surface work, a 3lb (1.3 Kg) leader is enough; any heavier, will tend to spoil presentation and be more visible. Any lighter, and the leader could break too easily. This could leave the unfortunate fish with a hook and yards of line trailing from it, which in turn, could get caught in the weed and so lead to its slow and painful demise.

Sub-surface fishing with large flies and lures calls for a 4lb (1.8 Kg) to 6lb (2.7 Kg) leader, and this will cover most eventualities. For really deep reservoir hunting, where you may be fishing down to depths of 100 feet (33m), then anything up to 10lb (4.5 Kg) will be necessary to overcome water tension on the line. The length of the leader is not too critical with 9ft (3m) for a lure or wet fly being average, and sometimes going out to 15ft (5m) for small, dry flies — the extra length to allow the fly to drop more gently onto the surface.

THE 'PRESENTATION'

If you stand by the waterside doing an impression of Mantovani conducting the Flight of the Bumble Bee with a fly rod, and perhaps dancing in and out of the water in waders, then you shouldn't be surprised if the fish are trying to clamber up the far bank in fright.

Keep a low profile, reducing false casts to a minimum, with slow and deliberate actions, think 'still'. Be especially careful if you can see the trout, because they are more than likely looking right back at you just as intently.

Sometimes, towards late evening, your cast can start crashing in a heap on the water. This is caused by the 'lift' going out of the air. Make shorter casts — the lift usually returns after sunset.

THE 'TAKE'

Keyword — CONCENTRATION. If you want to chat to your fellow angler, commune with nature, or respond to the environment — please do so. They are all extremely laudable pursuits. If, on the other hand, you want to catch more fish, then *concentrate.*

Tunnel your vision to the fly if you are fishing dry with a floating line, or to the end of the line if you are using nymphs, pupae or any wet fly. Do exactly the same in the case of a sinking line, but concentrate on the first two or three feet (1m) visible under water.

At the *slightest* hesitation, twitch, movement, or anything else which you even *consider* to be a take, tighten *immediately,* whether you *feel* a fish or *not.* The *only* exception to this rule is when fishing dry flies and long-tailed lures, such as nobblers and chenilles.

With a dry fly, after you see a take, count 3 seconds before lifting the rod; this gives the fish time to turn and dive, giving you a better chance of setting the hook. This, of course, is easier said than done, because 3 seconds seems like 3 hours and all your instincts are screaming

"STRIKE"!!!

In the case of a long-tailed lure, a fish will often nip at the tail several times before taking, producing a series of 'knocks'. Continue the retrieve until a sustained pull is felt and then tighten. Takes occuring during the retrieve can often be felt, but in the pauses between retrieves, or when the fly is fished static, usually the *only* indication of a take is line movement.

Some takes, however, can feel like an express train hitting — in this case the fish usually hook themselves.

Don't be too quick to lift the line out of the water in order to re-cast, instead, retrieve the last few feet, bringing the leader as close to the bank as possible whilst lifting the rod very slowly. Often, fish follow flies into the bank and take just as they are leaving the water.

. . . ALWAYS wet your hands before handling a fish.

THE LANDING

A well hooked trout is sometimes followed by a well rounded curse as the fish escapes whilst the angler is trying to net it.

The ancient truth that more fish are lost at the net than at any other time is oh, so accurate.

Trying to stab at the trout with your net like King Arthur and his Trusty Sword is likely to send the fish into Never Never Land, complete with your hook, line, and pride.

Far better to submerge your net, slowly bring the fish over it and lift sharply. Keep your rod arm fully extended so that if the fish makes a last second surge, it will act as a shock-absorber and help to foil the would-be escapee's ploy.

The secret is to play the fish for as long as it takes before you even consider using the net.

ALWAYS carry a 'priest' and ALWAYS carry forceps (disgorger) in case a fly is swallowed by the fish. If there is any doubt that a fish may be injured, it should be despatched.

THE WEED

Wonderful stuff weed. Lots of creepy crawlies live on, in, and under it. Trout love creepy crawlies. Most stillwaters are blessed with their fair share of weed, but some are over-blessed and this is when problems can occur.

Fishing a floating line with dry or wet flies to surface or near surface fish is fine, but when using a sinking line and slow retrieving, or 'inching' for bottom feeders, your best catch of the day can be 10lbs. of the very best variegated pond weed. Frustration!

There are several ways to overcome this annoyance. Try using a floating line with a long leader; the flies will then have a tendency to bounce over, rather than through the weed. Bushy flies can often help in these circumstances, as the hook is more protected — a Soldier Palmer is a good example.

Another method is to use an intermediate or slow sink line rather than a fast sinker. The latter will get flies down quicker but will also drag them through the weed. An intermediate or slow sink line descends less quickly, thereby allowing you to retrieve your line slowly, just above the weed, before it settles amongst it. The exact moment can be judged by counting in seconds from the moment the line hits the water, until it sinks to the weed bed. The time can easily be judged as it corresponds directly to the amount of weed dragged up by your fly! By counting a number of seconds before this occurs, the flies can be fished just above the danger zone.

THE CLIMATE

Varying climatic changes and the way they can affect fishing, is a little like the study of Astrology. There's an awful lot to learn, and having learned it all, it never seems to work out the way you think it should.

Generally speaking, in extremes of hot or cold weather, fish tend to bottom feed where the temperatures are fairly constant.

Barometric pressure also plays a significant role and there is some truth in the old saying 'When the glass rises, so do the fish. When the glass goes down, the fish follow'.

THE SIZE, SHAPE AND COLOUR

We're talking about the artificial flies and not the angler! Of these three, shape and colour are more important than size. If the shape of the artificial you are using looks like, or even vaguely resembles, a natural fly, your catching chances are greatly improved. Colour is of equal importance; very often when two flies are used with the same pattern, but varying in colour, you can find that one will achieve far greater results than the other. It pays to experiment.

Size is generally of lesser importance. The most popular hook sizes used by stillwater trout anglers are between 10 and 14. This makes an artificial midge pupa look like 'King Kong' compared to the real thing, but it doesn't seem to bother the trout over much, so long as it *looks* like a midge pupa.

THE WIND

When the wind blows, apart from rocking cradles, the fish tend to go with the flow and end up amongst the accumulations of flotsam and jetsam, looking for a meal. Try to cast into the wind. There are times when you will feel like Canute trying to reverse the tide, but perseverance can bring more fish than casting from the opposite and easier bank, with the wind behind you.

THE CHANGEOVER

Once a catching pattern is established and you're happily getting stuck into the fish, a strange thing can often happen. The fish suddenly stop taking your fly. Try as you may, they will simply ignore what was, up until a second ago, their favourite snack. Persist with the pattern as the fish may be shoaling and could return. If nothing happens, it could be that they've gone off the main course and started on the sweet.

In effect, this is probably the case. The fish suddenly decide to change over to another hatching delicacy and immediately ignore everything else. Be prepared for this occurrence, try and establish what the new food pattern is and change flies accordingly. Always exhaust the possibilities of a fly by trying different retrieves before changing patterns.

THE 'MATCH THE HATCH'

The old adage 'match the hatch' still rings as true today as ever it did. If a little, fluffy, green thing with white wings is fluttering about, try and fish something similar, or the nymph or pupa you think would be appropriate to it. The chances are it will work.

BUT don't be ruled by this saying. Sometimes a large, fat, red thing will work when the little, fluffy, green thing doesn't!

THE 'DROPPERS'

Fish at least two flies (point and dropper), or three (point, dropper and bob).

There are several sound reasons for this. Flies can be chosen and eliminated two or three times faster than using just a single fly. To begin with, it often pays to use totally opposite types of flies together, until a catching pattern is established. Unless you are a 'one fly man', or perhaps a beginner, it is suggested that the only time a single fly is used, is in poor light or windy conditions, when tangles can easily happen (and frequently do!) using teams of flies. As a guide, we suggest the droppers to be 3 feet (1 metre) apart and 6 inches (15 centimetres) long.

THE POSITION

Position is all important. If the fish aren't taking, don't anchor yourself to the one spot on the bank — move about; the fish do! To remain fishless in the same place for hours on end is illogical, boring, can be soul destroying, and is confidence-sapping. When confidence is undermined, mistakes can be made.

Try not to become a member of those serried ranks of immobile anglers, flogging away at the same patch of water all day. If you see a rise elsewhere — go for it. If you see fish being taken by other anglers, position yourself as close to them as etiquette and commonsense will allow.

Move around. This will stimulate the adrenalin for the challenge of pastures new. Your chances of success are greatly improved as every cast is made with renewed confidence.

THE ENVIRONMENT

Wildlife is having a hard enough time as it is without the additional problems caused by the thoughtless angler. Line is carelessly discarded when it takes only a matter of seconds to wind it round your fingers, tie a knot in it and pop it in your bag or pocket. These few seconds could well save a lot of misery or even the life of some birds or animals. The same goes for lead shot, plastic bags, and of course the inevitable beer can!

NATURAL

FLY

SECTION

NATURAL FLIES ETC.

THE FLIES HAVE BEEN LAID OUT TOGETHER, FOR INSTANT WATERSIDE IDENTIFICATION.

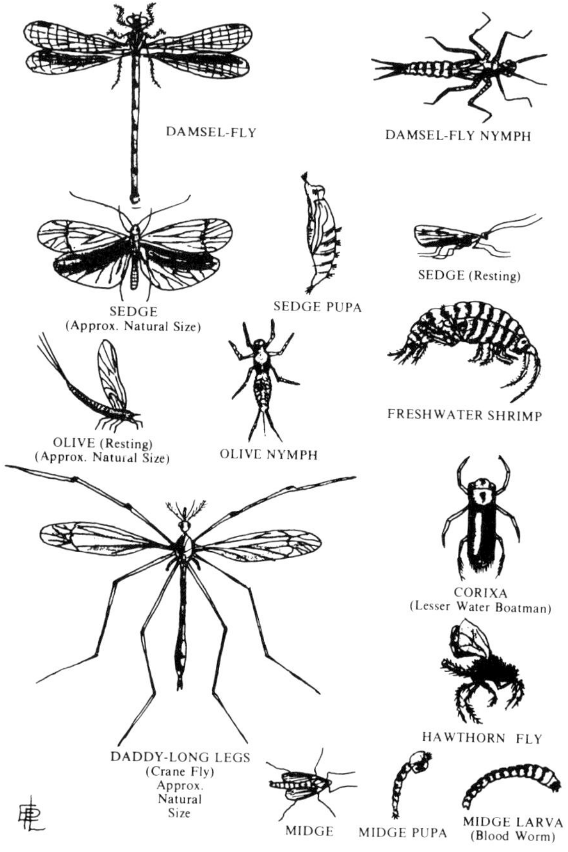

HATCHES

A hatch, in fly-fishing terms, happens at that part of the day, usually morning or evening, when particular species of fly decide to rise to the surface, shuck off their pupal cases and take flight. This they do as a Union, a case of 'one out, all out'. The trout, of course, consider this a feast and rise to the occasion — literally. Swimming amongst them, on or near the surface, they create splashes and rings as they avidly feed. Some of the finest (or most frustrating) fishing can occur at this time.

There are thousands of different types of flies that hatch in stillwaters but not all of them are of interest to the fly-fisher; the varieties we'll deal with, will include their complicated, tongue-twisting, Latin names, not to create confusion, but to enable you, if you feel up to it, to research more deeply into the subject — but in tomes far more weighty than ours!

Standing by the water's edge, with fish splashing about your feet, it is more important to know what the various flies actually *look* like than have a head full of Latin names.

We'll describe the types you are most likely to meet, with a typical example illustrated, together with corixa, shrimp and daddy-long-legs.

NATURAL FLIES ETC.

MIDGES *(Chironomids)*

Various hatchings throughout the year but mainly between May and September. These are the most prolific of all the flies mentioned and form a major part of a trout's diet. Midges are those pesky little flies that swarm around your ears in clouds and look like (and often bite like) mini-mosquitoes.

Flies to try. Midge Pupa, Chomper, Tups Indispensable, Pheasant Tail Nymph, Mallard and Claret, Greenwell's Glory, Grey Duster.

SEDGES *(Trichoptera)*

The Sedge or Caddis Fly appears mostly on warm summer afternoons and evenings throughout June to September. If you see a fluttery, moth-like fly with mottled brown wings, then more than likely there's a sedge hatch underway.

Flies to try. Sedge Pupa, Muddler Minnow, Pheasant Tail Nymph, Invicta, Mallard and Claret, Cinnamon Sedge.

DAMSEL-FLIES *(Zygoptera)*

Appearing between May and September, these beautiful flies with gorgeous iridescent wings of blue or green cruise above the surface like small Lancaster Bombers. They look a lot like their larger cousin the dragonfly.

Flies to try. Damselfly Nymph, Sedge Pupa, Muddler Minnow, Pheasant Tail Nymph, Invicta.

DADDY-LONG-LEGS *(Diptera)*

Mainly June to October. A very obvious fly, with long gangly legs and slender wings. These flies don't actually hatch from water, but because of their questionable aerobatics tend to get blown onto it anyway.

Flies to try. Daddy-long-legs, Invicta, Muddler Minnow.

CORIXA *(Hemiptera)*

Also known as the Lesser Water Boatman. Appears throughout the year. If you see what looks like a small, black-backed beetle dart up to the surface, grab a blob of air, and nip back down to the bottom — it's a corixa.

Flies to try. Corixa, Chomper and Shrimp.

CAENIS *(Ephemeroptera)*

The infamous 'angler's curse'. Mainly occuring between May and September. When fish are feeding and splashing away at a hatching of a particular type of tiny, white winged Olive Fly and ignoring everything you're putting in front of them, you're in the middle of a caenis hatch.

Flies to try. Hare's Ear Nymph, Chomper, Pheasant Tail Nymph, Midge Pupa, Greenwell's Glory, Grey Duster.

SHRIMP *(Gammarus)*

Throughout the year. Everyone should know that a shrimp is a small, arched backed creature with lots of short hairy legs! You'll often see them swimming in the margins.

Flies to try. Shrimp, Corixa, Chomper, Soldier Palmer.

OLIVES *(Ephemeroptera)*

Various hatchings from May to October. They look like tiny yachts serenely sailing along in a Sunday afternoon regatta.

Flies to try. Greenwell's Glory, Coachman, Black and Peacock Spider, Pheasant Tail Nymph, Gold Ribbed Hare's Ear, Grey Duster.

HAWTHORN FLY *(Diptera)*

In April and May when the hawthorn bush is usually in flower, these unwieldy black flies are blown onto the water.

Flies to try. Hawthorn Fly, Black & Peacock Spider, Black Pennell.

ARTIFICIAL

FLY

SECTION

FLY CHART

	PAGE	APR	MAY	JUN	JUL	AUG	SEP	OCT
CINNAMON SEDGE	45			X	X	X	X	
COACHMAN	47			X	X	X		
DADDY-LONG-LEGS	49			X	X	X	X	X
DAMSELFLY NYMPH	49		X	X	X	X	X	
GOLD RIBBED HARE'S EAR	51		X	X	X	X	X	X
GREY DUSTER	53		X	X	X	X	X	X
HAWTHORN FLY	55	X	X					
INVICTA	55			X	X	X		
MIDGE PUPA	57	X	X	X	X	X	X	X
MUDDLER MINNOW	59			X	X	X	X	
PHEASANT TAIL NYMPH	59		X	X	X	X	X	X
SEDGE PUPA	61			X	X	X	X	
TUPS INDISPENSABLE	63			X	X	X	X	
BLACK & PEACOCK SPIDER	43	THROUGHOUT YEAR						
BLACK PENNELL	43	THROUGHOUT YEAR						
CHOMPER	45	THROUGHOUT YEAR						
CORIXA	47	THROUGHOUT YEAR						
GREENWELL'S GLORY	51	THROUGHOUT YEAR						
HARE'S EAR NYMPH	53	THROUGHOUT YEAR						
MALLARD & CLARET	57	THROUGHOUT YEAR						
SHRIMP	61	THROUGHOUT YEAR						
SOLDIER PALMER	63	THROUGHOUT YEAR						

THE ABOVE CHART SUGGESTS APPROXIMATE MONTHS TO FISH THE FLIES, N.B. WEATHER CONDITIONS CAN ALTER THE HATCHING TIMES MARKEDLY, eg. A DADDY-LONG-LEGS WAS WITNESSED ON A NORTHERN FISHERY IN THE LAST WEEK OF APRIL.

THE ARTIFICIAL FLIES

The artificial flies can be loosely separated into four groups — Dry Flies, Wet Flies, Nymphs (including Pupae) and Lures.

There are ardent followers of each of these groups, who will fish virtually nothing but their chosen type, just as there are strict adherents to the floating line and those that prefer sinkers.

As our prime purpose is to help you catch more fish, we favour no particular type, but recommend the use of all, as and when circumstances dictate.

You will find that we use only a small percentage of dry flies, but we do so because the wet varieties tend to take more fish over a complete season, all things being equal.

The most popular, and generally recommended fly hook sizes to use are, 10 and 12, going smaller to sizes 14 and 16, for some dry flies, and larger to sizes 8 and 6, for lures, including nobblers.

There are numerous variations of traditional fly patterns; our selection shows the type readily available in tackle shops. They may not be to the standards of a fly dressing aficianado, but they work!

Black & Peacock Spider

Black Pennell

BLACK & PEACOCK SPIDER

Throughout the year.

Fish Rising: Use a FLOATING line, and fish dry allowing the fly to drift naturally, or use a slow retrieve. Can also be fished just below the surface film with a moderate speed retrieve.

No Rises: Use a FLOATING line, fish wet with slow 'sink & draw' technique, or use a SINKING line with a moderate retrieve.

BLACK PENNELL

Throughout the year.

A successful and well known pattern which can be used to represent spiders, hawthorne flies, gnats etc.

Fish Rising: Use a FLOATING line, and, with floatant on the leader, fish just sub-surface with a slow to medium speed retrieve.

No Rises: With a FLOATING line and long leader, use the 'sink & draw' method with medium speed retrieve. Use a SINKING line and a slow retrieve.

Chomper

Cinnamon Sedge

CHOMPER

Throughout the year.

A RICHARD WALKER creation and a great, all year, all weather, fly. Appears to represent several food patterns to the fish, including shrimp and corixa.

Fish Rising: Use a FLOATING line, with the fly 'twitched' or drawn steadily beneath the surface film, or cast into a rise ring, allow to sink, and retrieve slowly. Try during 'Angler's Curse'.

No Rises: 'Nymph' or inch slowly along the bottom, preferably with a SINKING line.

CINNAMON SEDGE

May through October.

As the name suggests, use in a sedge hatch. Well known and well used because it produces results.

Fish Rising: Use a FLOATING line and retrieve fairly slowly — just enough to create a wake. Also try leaving it to drift.

Coachman

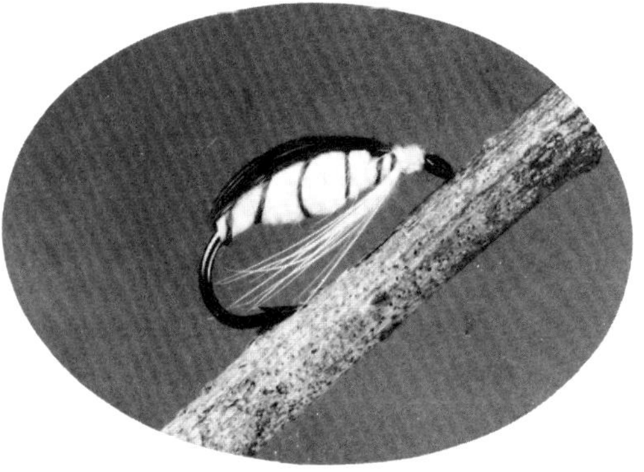

Corixa

COACHMAN

During June, July and August.

Not an imitative, but a basic up-wing fly which is very useful when there are flies on the water. On hot summer's days and warm evenings, when Olives are hatching, an excellent choice, which should take its fair share of fish.

Fish Rising: Use a FLOATING line with a very slow, and occasionally 'twitchy', retrieve.

CORIXA

Throughout the year.

Rise or No Rise: Use a FLOATING line, allow the fly to sink naturally and then, with a slow draw technique, gently bring up to the surface. With a SINKING line, use a *floating* corixa. Allow the line to sink to the bottom, then use a medium draw with intermittent pauses.

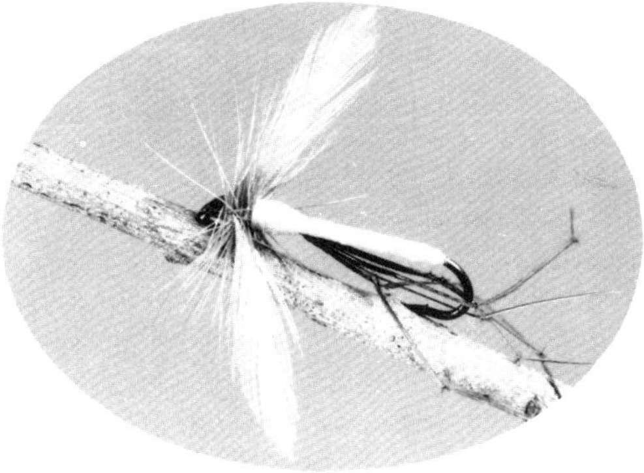

Daddy-long-legs

Damselfly Nymph

DADDY-LONG-LEGS

June through to October are the months for this one.

Fish it dry on a FLOATING line. You cast it and you leave it — perhaps the odd twitch now and again. If it sinks, let it — many fish have been caught as it slowly sinks to the bottom.

DAMSELFLY NYMPH

Mid-May through September.

An excellent nymph when the beautifully coloured Damselflies (bright blues, greens, and sometimes, reds) and their bigger, drabber brothers, the dragonflies, are on the wing. Both nymphs are fairly similar and trout don't seem to discriminate too much.

Fish Rising: Use a FLOATING line, let the nymph sink to the bottom, and slowly 'tweak' back to the surface, or, use a medium draw with the nymph in the surface film.

No Rises: Use a SINKING line, and draw slowly along the bottom.

With a FLOATING line, use the 'sink and draw' method.

Gold-Ribbed Hare's Ear

Greenwell's Glory

GOLD-RIBBED HARE'S EAR

May through October.

One of the best representatives of the Olive Dun and it's been around a long, long time. Use in a Olive hatch.

Fish Rising: Use a FLOATING line, cast into the ring of a rise and retrieve with sufficient speed to create a shallow wake. Make sure your landing net is handy!

GREENWELL'S GLORY

March through October.

Best loved of the old fly patterns, and found in nearly every fly-box. Representative of up-wing flies.

Fish Rising: During an Olive hatch, use a FLOATING line. Cast out a dry fly, and let it drift — the occasional brief 'twitch' sometimes stimulates action. When fished wet, use the 'sink & draw' method, or fish fairly fast just below the surface.

No Rises: Best to use a FLOATING line and the 'sink & draw' method. Its popularity is not an accident. Canon Greenwell lives on!

Grey Duster

Hare's Ear Nymph

GREY DUSTER

May through October.

An extremely useful little fly this one, particularly in an Olive hatch, or a frustrating attack of 'angler's curse'!

Fish Rising: Use a FLOATING line. Cast out the dry fly and leave it to drift — give it the occasional 'twitch'. Also try a medium speed draw, creating a shallow wake, especially during 'angler's curse'.

HARE'S EAR NYMPH

Throughout the year.

An old favourite and all-rounder.

Fish Rising: Use a FLOATING line, and strip fairly fast below surface film, or use a line floatant, and fish slowly in the surface film. Effective during 'Angler's Curse' or Olive hatch. Try the 'sink & draw' method.

No Rises: A SINKING line can be used, with a long slow draw, or, the nymph can be inched, slowly along the bottom. Also try a short, fast, 'jerky' draw.

Hawthorne Fly

Invicta

HAWTHORN FLY

April & May.

Use when you see these ugly black flies with their long, trailing back legs.

Fish Rising: Use a FLOATING line and fish dry, allowing the artificial to drift, or use a slow retrieve 'stop/start' method, to stimulate a take. Still on the floating line, fish wet, using the 'sink & draw' technique.

If you haven't got a Hawthorn Fly artificial, use a similar black fly pattern, eg. Black & Peacock Spider.

INVICTA

June, July and August.

One of the best artificial flies to use during a sedge hatch.

Fish Rising: Use a FLOATING line and fish with a very slow retrieve in the surface film. Still on the floating line, use the 'sink & draw' technique.

Mallard & Claret

Midge Pupa

MALLARD & CLARET

Throughout the year.

A superb all round fly, which does not represent anything in particular, apart from a tasty snack for trout.

Fish Rising: Use a FLOATING line and the 'long, slow draw' method, with a few occasional twitches, and the fly a couple of inches beneath the surface.

No Rises: Use a SINKING line and either inch along the bottom, or draw fairly quickly through the water.

Use either a floating or sinking line and fish at medium speed in mid-water to act as a lure. Try it on a cold day, medium speed, near the bottom.

MIDGE PUPA

April through October.

The obvious choice in a midge hatch.

Fish Rising: Use a FLOATING line with the 'sink & draw' method. Cast in to the ring of a rise. Remember, midge pupae cannot swim, they float to the surface and bob up and down. Try to imitate.

No Rises: Use a SINKING line and trundle slowly along the bottom.

Muddler Minnow

Pheasant Tail Nymph

MUDDLER MINNOW

June, July, August and September.

Strictly a lure, but one of the few capable of being fished on the surface. Imitative of virtually any moving fly on the water.

Fish Rising: Use a FLOATING line with a medium-speed draw to create a wake.

No Rises: Still on the floating line, use a medium-speed draw as this often stimulates a rise. Especially effective during a sedge hatch. Use a SINKING line and fish 'lure-like' along the bottom.

PHEASANT TAIL NYMPH

May through October.

The fish seem to take this nymph for several kinds of food. Extremely useful during the various hatches.

Fish Rising: Use a FLOATING line and strip fairly fast through, or just below the surface film. Try the 'sink & draw' method at medium speed. Also try a short, fast, 'jerky' draw.

No Rises: Use a SINKING line and trundle slowly along the bottom. This is an old favourite and a sure catcher.

Sedge Pupa

Shrimp

SEDGE PUPA

June, July, August & September.

The first choice during a sedge hatch. Doctor Bell's amber nymph is among the best of the artificials.

Fish Rising: Use a FLOATING line and either, allow the pupa to sink to the bottom and draw steadily back to the surface, or retrieve at medium speed, just beneath the surface film. It also proves very effective when fished on the surface (using floatant), and stripped back to create a wake.

No Rises: Still using the floating line, fish the 'sink & draw' method. Use a SINKING line and fish slowly along the bottom with frequent pauses.

SHRIMP

Throughout the year.

Shrimps are found in most still-waters in abundance (providing the water is not 'acid') and provide trout with a regular food source. Fish on a SINKING line very slowly along the bottom.

With a FLOATING line and using a long leader, allow the shrimp to sink to the bottom, and use a slow, 'twitching' retrieve.

Soldier Palmer

Tups Indispensable

SOLDIER PALMER

Throughout the year.

Represents a variety of food patterns including sedge pupae.

Fish Rising: Use a FLOATING line and a slow 'sink & draw' technique. In a sedge hatch, cast and retrieve immediately (muddler-style).

No Rises: Still using a floating line allow the fly to sink and then retrieve very slowly with prolonged pauses.

Use a SINKING line, inching along the bottom, or use a long slow draw with frequent pauses.

TUPS INDISPENSABLE

June, July, August and September.

Last but not least in our list. A catching pattern for many, many, years.

Fish Rising: Use a FLOATING line and fish 'greased' nymph in the surface film. Allow to drift and give it the odd twitch now and again. Try also a fairly fast retrieve across the surface. With a 'degreased' nymph use the 'sink & draw' method. Use in an Olive or Angler's Curse hatch.

No Rises: Use a SINKING line and inch along the bottom, with frequent pauses.

LURES

ACE OF SPADES SWEENEY TODD

NOBBLER

BABY DOLL APPETISER

LURES (INCLUDING NOBBLERS)

These can prove devastating when used at the *right times,* but they are often treated as the absolute panacea, being first choice fly on all occasions, and sometimes used to the exclusion of all others.

There is no doubt that lures catch fish, but consider the fish you may fail to catch by not diversifying. Treat the lure as just another member of your fly-box and use accordingly.

The standard way of retrieving a lure seems to be the long, fast draw, or 'stripping' technique. Trout will take using this method, perhaps out of aggression or maybe curiosity, as is sometimes thought. Try 'inching', or a short, slow draw/pause, along the bottom We think you will be pleasantly surprised! Numerous trout have been taken using this method and there is no doubt in our minds that the fish consider the lure to be a food item, and most probably, fish fry.

N.B. Some 'takes' can be very gentle so beware!

The time to use a lure is when the obvious food patterns fail to work, or as part of a fly team with the lure on the point and food patterns further up — this is called "hedging your bets"!

Another obvious time is during 'dead' parts of the day, when no fish are showing, and very few, if any, are being caught.

It has been said that you should use a "bright lure on a bright day" and a "dark lure on a dull day" — this ain't necessarily so!!! We have often found the opposite to be the case.

IN CONCLUSION . . . .

Be a Fisherman not a Fishmonger!

In competition, it is the amount of fish caught that counts, but if points were given for skill, style, presentation, courtesy and, above all, sportsmanship, then some score-boards would be radically altered!

The real joy and pleasure of fly fishing is not playing the 'numbers and size' game, but to enjoy the sport for its own sake.

It means . . .

changing the flies when a fish has been caught instead of using the same one all day, "because it works".

It means . . .

fishing the *least* likely place on a stillwater you use regularly, and where you know all the best 'lies'.

It means . . .

returning the fish if you already have a healthy supply in the freezer!

It means . . .

testing your skill and knowledge to the limit to entice a fish — but think of the challenge!

Catching that single trout after stalking it for half an hour and, by your own craft and ingenuity, deceiving it into taking your "well dissembled fly", fills you with more satisfaction than if you were hauling in fish after fish on a lure.

This may appear to be in contradiction to the main purpose of this book but we believe it to be a natural progression. Having reached a level of understanding in the Art, and it is an Art, whereby you know what to use, when to use it, and how, more fish will come your way. You can then extend beyond the mere stockpiling of the deep-freeze to develop an awareness of the true enjoyment of fly-fishing, and indeed, of all sport.

IT'S NOT WHETHER YOU WIN OR LOSE,
BUT HOW YOU PLAY THE GAME.

MONTHLY NOTES

January

February

March MIDGE Pupae, CADDIS, SHRIMP, SNAIL

April AS ABOVE

May MIDGE Pupae, OLIVES, CORIXA.

June MIDGE Pupae, OLIVES, DAMSEL, SEDGE, CAENIS.

MONTHLY NOTES

July Midge Pupae, Sedge, Damsel, Caenis, Snails, Later Corixa

---

August As Above.

September Midge Pupae, Corixa, Snails Olives, Fry Feeding

October Midge Pupae, Corixa, Fry Feeding

November

December

GENERAL NOTES

BLACK MIDGE	JUL, AUG, SEPT (2ND ½)
LARGE GREEN	JUL (2ND ½) AUG
LARGE RED	JUNE (2ND ½) JULY, AUG SEPT (1ST ½)
RIBBED MIDGE	MAY, JUNE AUG (2ND ½), SEPT
SMALL BLACK	END JUNE THRU TO BEGIN SEPT
SMALL RED	JULY, AUGUST, SEPT

HOOK	SIZE	NYLON
L/S	6-8	6 lb.
L/S	8-10	5 lb.
ST	8-12	5 lb
L/S	10-12	4 lb
ST	10-14	4 lb
ST	10-16	3 lb
ST	14-20	2 lb

GENERAL NOTES

Power-Gum

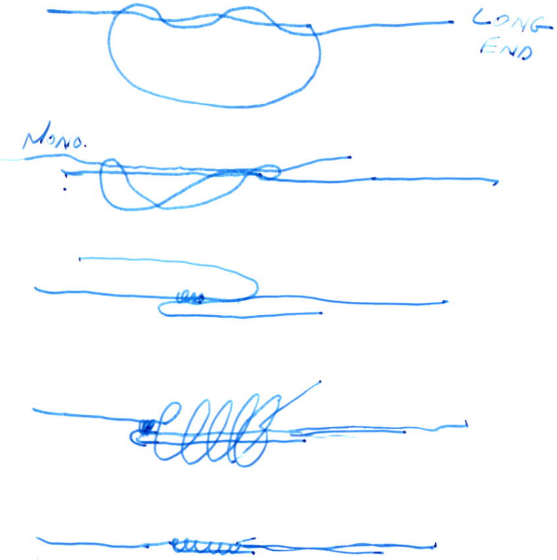